Insects Activity Book

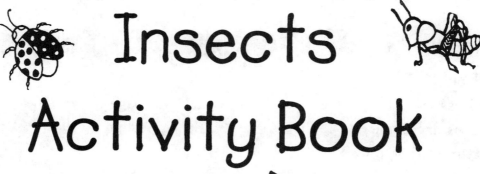

Author	Ellen Sussman
Editor	Kathy Rogers
Illustrator	Barb Lorseyedi
Page Design	Linda Milliken
Cover Design	Imaginings

METRIC CONVERSION CHART
Refer to this chart when metric conversions are not found within the activity.

¼ tsp.	=	1.25 ml	350° F	=	175° C
½ tsp.	=	2.5 ml	375° F	=	190° C
1 tsp.	=	5 ml	400° F	=	200° C
1 Tbsp.	=	15 ml	425° F	=	220° C
¼ cup	=	60 ml	1 inch	=	2.54 cm
⅓ cup	=	75 ml	1 foot	=	30 cm
½ cup	=	125 ml	1 yard	=	91 cm
1 cup	=	230 ml	1 mile	=	1.6 km
		1 oz.	=	28 g	
		1 lb.	=	.45 kg	

EP115 • ©1998, 2004 Edupress, Inc.™ • P.O. Box 883 • Dana Point, CA 92629
www.edupressinc.com
ISBN 1-56472-115-9
Printed in USA

Table of Contents

Glossary

antennae—feelers located between the eyes on some insects; used for smelling and feeling.

beetle—an insect that has two pairs of wings; the hard front wings cover the thin hind wings when the hind wings are folded.

caterpillar—the larva of a butterfly or moth.

chitin—one of the substances that makes up an insect's exoskeleton.

cocoon—the silky case that caterpillars spin to shelter themselves while they are changing into butterflies or moths.

compound eyes—large eyes made of many separate lenses; most insects have compound eyes.

chrysalis—the pupa of a butterfly or moth.

colony—a group of animals or plants living or growing together.

drone—a male honeybee; it does no work and has no sting.

entomologist—a scientist who studies insects.

exoskeleton—a stiff shell that covers an insect's body and protects it.

larva—a young insect that does not look like its parents.

mandibles—powerful grinding jaws of an insect; they work from side-to-side, not up-and-down as in humans.

metamorphosis—the change in form as an insect develops into an adult.

mimics—an insect that is protected by its close appearance to an insect with protective devices.

molting—the process of shedding the outgrown exoskeleton as an insect grows.

nectar—a sweet liquid inside a flower which attracts insects.

nurses—insects within a colony that take care of the young.

nymph—a young insect that resembles its parents.

ocelli—simple eyes that are set between an insect's compound eyes; they can only tell the difference between light and dark.

ovipositor—egg-laying body part of a female insect; used to insert eggs into things like soil, wood, or leaves.

pollinate—to place pollen on the pistil of a flower.

proboscis—a long, flexible tube used by an insect to suck nectar.

protective coloration—coloring that protects a plant or animal from its enemies.

pupa—the stage in an insect's life between larva and adult.

queen—the only egg-laying female in a nest of social insects such as ants and bees.

social insect—an insect that lives in an organized community with other insects.

soldiers—insects within a colony that are responsible for defending against attacks by enemies.

stridulating—the sound an insect makes by rubbing one part of the body against another.

swarm—a large number of bees, led by a queen, leaving a hive to start a new colony.

thorax—the middle section of an insect's body.

wrigglers—the larvae of mosquitoes.

Glossary Game

After learning many interesting facts about insects, see if you know what these words mean. Draw a line to connect each word to its definition.

Exoskeleton

a sweet liquid inside a flower which attracts insects

Antennae

the change in form as an insect develops into an adult

Nymph

an insect that lives in an organized community with other insects

Metamorphosis

the larva of a moth or butterfly

Larva

a long, flexible tube used by an insect to suck nectar

Social Insect

the only egg-laying female in a nest of social insects such as ants and bees

Nectar

a stiff shell that covers an insect's body and protects it

Queen

the stage in an insect's life between larva and adult

Caterpillar

the pupa of a butterfly or moth

Pupa

feelers located between the eyes on some insects and used for smelling and feeling

Chrysalis

a young insect that does not look like its parents

Proboscis

a young insect that resembles its parents

Score: If you got all 12 correct, you are in insect expert!
If you got 10-11 correct, you've learned a lot about insects.
If you got 9 or fewer correct, you're not an insect lover.

Introduction to Insects

An insect is a small, air-breathing, six-legged animal. Ants, bees, butterflies, cockroaches, crickets, fireflies, grasshoppers, houseflies, ladybugs, mosquitoes, moths, and wasps are insects. Scientists say there are over 800,000 kinds of insects!

A spider is not an insect. A spider's body has two parts; an insect's body has three. Spiders have eight legs; insects have six. Most insects have wings and antennae but spiders do not.

An insect's body has three main parts: the *head*, the *thorax*, and the *abdomen*. The *skeleton* of an insect is on the outside and is called an *exoskeleton*. It protects the internal organs. The muscles that work the legs and wings are attached to the inside of the thorax.

Insects are often classified into two groups: beneficial and harmful. Beneficial insects include those that help pollinate plants and flowers such as bees, wasps, flies, butterflies, and moths. Harmful insects include those that attack and feed on plants such as the boll weevil, corn earworm, carpet beetle, and gypsy moth, and pests such as termites and mosquitoes. Some insects can be beneficial in one way and harmful in another. It is important to remember that while insects feed on plants and animals, they also are food for plants and animals. This helps maintain the balance of the total number of plants and animals on Earth.

Much of the success of insects is due to their powers of reproduction. Although they have short lives, they quickly become adults, reproduce, and lay many eggs. Many kinds of insects can produce several generations in one season.

To get started on the study of insects, use these starting points:

 Take a walk in the neighborhood and look for insects—under rocks and logs, on plants, in between cracks in the sidewalk, by a pond, on trees. Identify as many as you can.

 Make a list of all the insects you can name. Are the insects you know about beneficial or harmful?

 Visit a children's museum and examine enlarged models of insects.

 Collect and label photographs of insects of all kinds.

 Set up a class library rich with books on all kinds of insects.

Ants

Information

Ants—like bees, wasps, and termites—are insects that live and work together in organized communities. Therefore they are known as *social insects*. A community of social insects is called a *colony*. Each colony has one or several *queens* whose chief job is to lay eggs. Most members of a colony are *workers* who are also female. They build the nest, search for food, care for the young, and fight enemies. The only job of the males is to mate with the queen.

All ants work together to maintain an ant colony. An ant hill is made from digging dirt from underground. Ants are great diggers and builders. An ant hill can be two feet (.6 meters) high and six feet (1.83 meters) wide.

Although ants are tiny, they are extremely strong. Most ants can lift objects that are ten times their body weight. Some ants can lift objects that are 50 times their weight.

Project

- Make ant farms.
- Experiment to see what foods attract ants.
- Complete an ant-fact challenge.

Materials

- Four glass jars
- Strainer
- Cheesecloth
- String
- Soil or sand
- Pieces of sponge
- Food—seeds, insects, sugar
- Ants
- All About Ants, following
- Resource books

Directions

1. Wash out glass jars. Sift soil into each jar. Fill them about two-thirds full of slightly moistened soil.

2. Put a small piece of damp sponge in each jar. The ants will use this as their source of water.

3. Using one empty jar, collect some ants. If you want the ant farms to last, search for a queen for each jar. (She will be two to three times larger than many worker ants.)

4. Put a few seeds in one jar, some dead insects in another, and some sugar in the last one. Too much food is not good for ants.

5. Tie some cheesecloth over the top of each jar to let air in and keep the ants from getting out.

6. Keep the ant farms in a dark place to simulate living underground. Bring them out into the light to watch the ants. Add a few drops of water as needed with a medicine dropper.

7. Are the ants in one jar surviving better than in the other two jars? If so, why? Draw conclusions about ants from your observations.

8. Use resource books to complete All About Ants.

All About Ants

Ants are divided into three main groups—queens, workers, and males.
Read about each group and list the main jobs and habits of each.

Queen Ants

Jobs: _____
_____
_____

Habits: _____
_____
_____

Worker Ants

Jobs: _____
_____
_____

Habits: _____
_____
_____

Male Ants

Jobs: _____
_____
_____

Habits: _____
_____
_____

Which ants have the harder jobs? Do male or female ants work the hardest? Draw a
conclusion and make a list of facts to support your answer.

Insects Activity Book

© Edupress EP115

Ant Anatomy

Information

An ant's body has three main parts: the head, the trunk, and the *metasoma*. The internal organs and sense organs are similar to those of many other insects.

An ant's chief sense organs are its two *antennae* which are attached to the front of the head. Ants use the antennae for smell, touch, taste, and hearing. When an ant is active, the antennae move almost constantly. They pick up scents in the air, search for and examine food, and find their way about with antennae.

An ant has three pair of legs which are attached to the bottom of the trunk.

The metasoma has two parts: the waist and the larger part, the *gaster*. Some ants have a poisonous sting at the tip of the gaster.

Project

- Work in groups to build a papier mâché ant.
- Complete one or more art or craft projects related to an ant's anatomy.

Materials

- Flour, water, newspaper for papier mâché
- Long balloons
- Tempera paint & brushes
- Construction paper
- Pipe cleaners
- Glue
- Aprons or smocks
- Scissors
- Cardboard
- Large photographs of ants

Directions

1. Set up work tables and divide into groups of four to five students.

2. Each group decides on the scale or size of the model they are going to make. Working from photographs, each child in the group creates one part of the ant model.

3. Use convex parts of long balloons to create main body parts using papier mâché.

4. Allow to dry. Cut into shapes for each part and paint.

5. Use pipe cleaners for legs and antennae. Attach legs to trunk. Connect all body parts. Add eyes.

6. Label external parts.

7. Display finished ant models.

Ant Art

Try these awesome "ant art" ideas!

Splatter Ants

Dip a **brush** into **black paint**. Stand back and with the tip of your finger, splatter the paint onto a piece of **paper**. Use each black splatter to create an ant. Add legs, antennae, eyes. How many ants can you make from one splatter?

Spongy Ants

Cut **sponges** into small pieces for the head and longer ones for the trunk and metasoma. Dip into **black paint.** Sponge onto **paper** to create likeness of ants. Add legs and antennae with **crayons** or **markers**. Use for a bulletin board border.

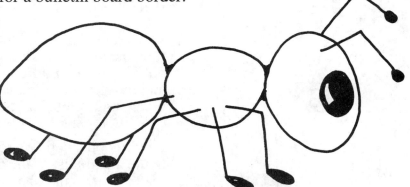

Picnic-Partner Ants

Since every picnic has ants, use the pattern below to make picnic napkin rings! Trace pattern onto **black construction paper**. Carefully cut out. Add legs and antennae with **pipe cleaners** or narrow strips of construction paper. Roll and twist one pipe cleaner to form the napkin ring. Attach finished ant pattern to napkin ring. Children may make enough for their family or have a class picnic outdoors and use them.

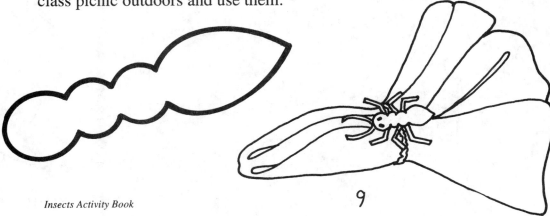

Bees

Information

Bees are one of nature's most useful insects as they help to pollinate plants. They produce honey and beeswax, two very useful products for people.

Flowers provide food for bees. The bees collect tiny grains of pollen and a sweet liquid called nectar from blossoms on plants. Bees make honey from the nectar and use both honey and pollen as food. As bees fly about and gather this food from plants, they spread pollen from one flower to another. This pollinates, or fertilizes, the plants they visit and enables the plants to reproduce. Flower plants, as well as fruit and vegetable plants, depend on bees for fertilization.

Project

Complete a chart showing the similarities and differences of a variety of bees.

Materials

- Books and photographs on several varieties of bees
- Busy As a Bee chart, following

Directions

1. Arrange a visit to an outdoor park with flowers, a municipal or private garden, or to a beekeeper for children to see how bees live and move about. Contact a local nursery for other suggestions in your area where children can observe bees safely.

2. Read independently about different bees. Make a class list of the different kinds of bees read about. Which bee makes enough honey and beeswax to be used by people?

3. Reproduce the Busy as a Bee chart. Complete the chart as a class, library, or homework activity.

Busy as a Bee!

Type of Bee	Hive or Nest Habits	Solitary or Social Bee	Stinging Habits
Honeybees			
Bumblebees			
Leafcutting Bees			
Mason Bees			
Burrowing Bees			

Honeybees

Information

A typical honey bee colony, called a hive, consists of one queen, tens of thousands of female workers, and a few hundred male bees called drones. The queen's only job is to lay eggs. Worker bees collect pollen and nectar as food and feed the young bees in the hive. They also clean the hive, produce wax, build cells of wax in the honeycomb, and guard it.

Honey is made by the worker bees from the sweet juice, or nectar, of flowers. Part of the process of making honey takes place in the bee's body and part in the hive. When honey is made, the bees eat some of it. The rest is stored in the honeycomb cells. Beekeepers collect honey from the combs, but they leave enough to feed the bees.

Project

- Collect items that contain beeswax.
- Taste a variety of honey flavors.

Materials

- Beeswax candles
- Samples of items with beeswax listed as an ingredient: crayons, lipstick, gum
- Samples of different flavored honey
- Bread

Directions

1. Explain that because beeswax burns slowly and gives off a pleasant smell, it makes good candles. Bring in a sample of a beeswax candle and smell it in its natural state. Then, using caution and a safe distance from the students, light the candle. Allow it to burn a while. Is the scent noticed? Is it different or the same as the scent of the candle before it was lit?

2. Look for labels on items that contain beeswax. Read the fine print on products such as chewing gum, crayons, adhesives, polishes, lipstick, and other cosmetics. Bring in samples for display. Explain why beeswax is an effective material for these products.

3. Have a "Honey Party." Bring in samples of honey. What different flavors are there? Spread on bread and sample the different tastes. For a theme touch, dress in yellow and black like bees!

Be a Bee!

Circle Dance

When a worker bee finds nectar and pollen, she shares it with the other bees in the hive. Soon they all head for the same places to find more. How do the bees know where to go?

The worker who has found the food does a special dance when she returns to the hive. The kind of dance she does shows the other bees the direction of the food. A bee will dance in a circle when the source of food is near the hive. In another dance, the bee buzzes and wags her body and makes a figure-eight pattern. This is called a wag-tail dance and is done when food is more than 27 yards (25 meters) from the hive.

Follow the directional pattern to simulate the circle dance of a worker bee. Buzz and try the wag-tail dance. Provide treats as food to the dancing bees!

Draw conclusions about why bees communicate in this way.

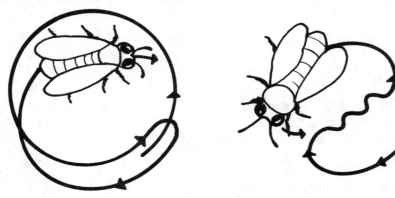

Spelling Bee

Have an ultimate spelling bee! Divide class into three teams: queens, workers, and drones. Using the glossary on page four, create a list of "bee vocabulary" words and have a unique spelling bee. Include words such as: honeycomb, pollen, hive, nectar, flower, buzz, queen, worker, drone, beeswax, beekeeper, sting.

Crickets

Information

A cricket is a type of jumping insect related to grasshoppers. They are usually found in pastures and meadows. They eat plants and the remains of other insects.

Crickets are well-known for the chirping sounds, or songs, they make. Male crickets chirp as a way of calling the female crickets to them. Most females cannot chirp. Each kind of cricket has a different "song," usually trills or a series of chirps. The male cricket does not chirp with his voice but by rubbing his two front wings together to make the chirping sound.

A cricket's ears are located under the knees of the front legs! Each ear is a tiny hole with a thin cover. Female crickets hear chirping sounds through these tiny holes.

Project

- Experiment to simulate the chirping sounds of crickets.
- Attempt to jump the equivalent distance of a cricket.

Materials

- Masking tape
- Metal nail files or woodshop files
- Sheets of cardboard
- Pieces of stiff plastic and metal

Directions

Like all insects, crickets have three pair of legs. The two front pair are small, but the back legs are longer and strong. Crickets use them to fly and to leap away from danger. Some crickets can leap about two feet (.6 m) which is about as far as a child can jump.

1. Use a blacktop surface or the floor of an indoor play area.

2. Use masking tape and lay out a six-foot (1.8 m) strip on the floor. Mark off every two feet *(.6 m)*.

3. Start at one mark and see how far can you jump. Can you jump from one mark to the next? Can some children jump farther? Who can jump the farthest? Why do you think some children are able to jump farther than others?

Like a Cricket!

Chirp...

Crickets use their front wings to create chirping sounds. Each wing has a sharp edge known as the *scraper* and a bumpy part called a *file.* The chirping sound is made by rubbing the scraper of one wing against the file of the other wing.

Pretend to be male crickets. Holding a piece of cardboard or other stiff paper, rub a metal file against the paper's edge. This sound closely resembles a cricket's chirp. Experiment using different thicknesses and types of paper to see how this affects the sound.

What conclusions can you draw about why different thicknesses of paper produce a different sound? Experiment further by rubbing a file against other materials such as a piece of plastic or metal. How is the sound different? What general conclusions can you draw from this activity?

...Chirp!

Depending on the season and your region, perhaps you can catch a cricket to study for a day or two. Use a big jar or plastic container and add about an inch of soil. Poke some air holes in the lid. At night, try to gently tap a cricket into the container. Once home, drop in bits of lettuce, moist bread crumbs, or a bit of honey. Add one section from an egg carton for the cricket to hide and feel safe in. Observe the cricket jumping around and eating. Listen for chirps. Release the cricket after a day or two in the same place where it was found. Why do you think a cricket would feel more secure with the protection of a section of egg carton when it already has the protection of an enclosed jar?

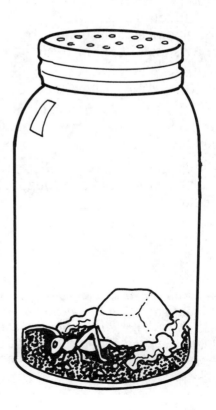

Crickets Close Up

Information

Several parts of a cricket's body have special uses. The rear legs are long and are used to leap and fly away from danger. The long antennae help the cricket to feel and smell its surroundings and find food. In most crickets, the antennae are much longer than the body.

Ears, under the knees of the front legs, help it to hear and to sense danger. The front wings are used by the male crickets to make chirping sounds, while the back wings are used for flying.

The cricket's strong jaw enables it to tear up leaves and insects for food.

Project

Label the diagram of a cricket's body with the name of each part and learn the function of each.

Materials

- Enlarged photographs of crickets
- Library and reference books
- Parts of a Cricket diagram, following

Directions

1. Visit a nature center or children's museum that has large models of insects and perhaps crickets, or invite a speaker from a local nature center to come and speak to the class about crickets.

2. Study photographs of crickets. Point out and discuss the functions of:
    - the file and scraper on the front wings
    - the ears under the knees on the front legs
    - the long back legs
    - the antennae

3. Reproduce the Parts of a Cricket diagram. Label each part in the box and write its function on the lines beside each part.

4. Display labeled crickets on a bulletin board. Set any jars of crickets you may have caught alongside the bulletin board.

For an extra activity, read Pinocchio to the class. Select a version with good illustrations. Does Jiminy Cricket resemble a cricket? In what ways?

Parts of a Cricket

Label each part of the cricket's body in the box. Tell what
the part is used for on the lines.

Back Legs

_____

_____

_____

Front Wings

_____

_____

_____

Antennae

_____

_____

_____

Jaw/Mouth

_____

_____

_____

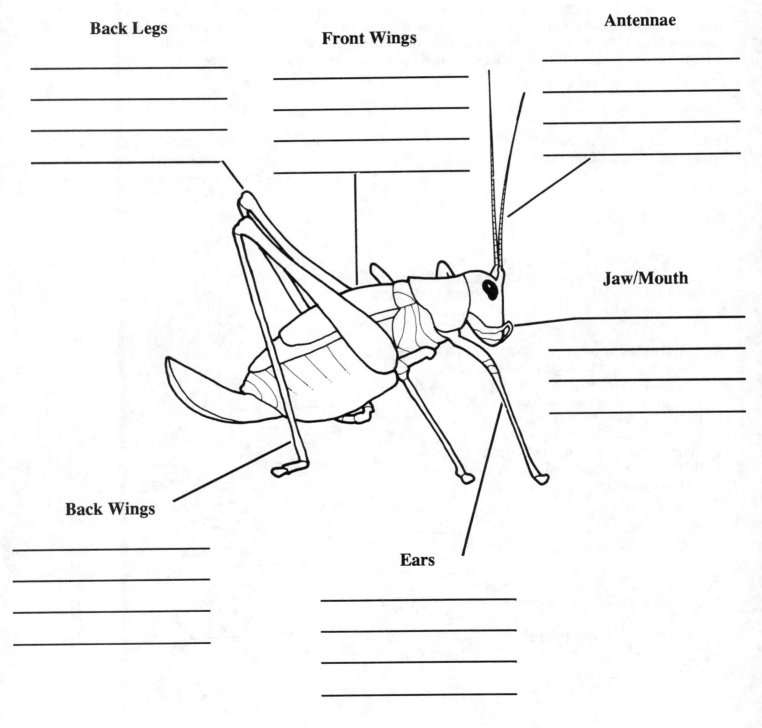

Back Wings

_____

_____

_____

Ears

_____

_____

_____

Insects Activity Book

Grasshoppers

Grasshoppers are famous for their jumping ability. They can leap about 20 times the length of their body. This feature often helps grasshoppers escape from enemies as it leaps up and flies away to safety. It can also defend itself against enemies by using its strong jaw and biting.

Grasshoppers can hide from enemies by blending in with their surroundings. Grasshoppers that live mainly near the ground are usually brown; grasshoppers that live near the beach are often sand-colored; those that live in grassy meadows and among leaves are usually green. In this way, nature has helped to protect grasshoppers from their predators—snakes, lizards, birds, mice, and other insects.

Project

Experiment with insect camouflage and protective coloration.

Materials

- Sheets of various construction paper in these colors: black, yellow, red, white, and green
- Pieces of same colored paper cut into pieces approximately two inches (5 cm) square

Directions

1. Discuss nature's way of protecting some animals by having them blend in with their surroundings. What animals can you name that have the ability to use their coloring to protect themselves?

2. Stand at the front of the room and hold up a large piece of black construction paper. Place a square of yellow, red, or white paper against it. Can the contrast be seen easily? Replace the paper square with a black one. Can you see the contrast now? Why is it easy to see one color against a contrasting background? Why is it difficult to notice a color against a background of the same color?

3. Repeat this using different colors—white against red; red against red; green against green; green against yellow, etc. Vary the distances.

4. Is it easier or harder to see one color against the same color background close-up? Why do you think so? What conclusions can you draw about an animal's ability to defend and protect itself by existing in an environment similar to its own color?

18

Grasshopper Environment

Project

Create a natural setting environment to show how grasshoppers of different colors blend in with their surroundings.

Materials

- Grasshopper patterns, below
- Natural materials such as grass blades, rocks, soil (see # 2)
- Glass dish   • Crayons or markers
- Pencil   • Scissors

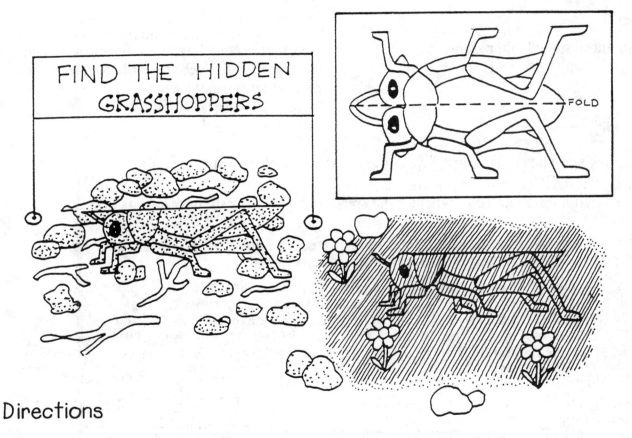

Directions

1. Divide into groups of three. Using the grasshopper pattern above, color one grass-green or leaf-green, one tan like sand, and one brown like soil. Cut each one out.

2. Gather materials from nature such as blades of grass, leaves, soil, rocks, twigs, sand, and extras like seashells and small flowers for a realistic touch.

3. In a small box or glass dish, arrange collected materials—all in the same color range—in a natural setting. Add the grasshopper to blend in so it isn't easy to see.

4. Set up a display table. Add a sign: Find the Hidden Grasshoppers! Invite another class in to view the displays. How easily can the visiting children find the hidden grasshoppers?

Spiracles

Information

The body of a grasshopper has some unique features. When it flies, the downstroke of the wings give the insect "lift" and moves it forward. The upstroke helps keep the grasshopper moving until the wings reach the downstroke position.

The grasshopper breathes by means of ten pairs of breathing holes called *spiracles* which are located in the lower part of the abdomen. Air enters through four spiracles nearest the head, and air leaves through the remaining six spiracles. Sometimes a grasshopper may overshoot its landing position and end up in a pond or lake. It must get out of the water quickly or it will drown as water enters through the four air-intake spiracles near its head.

Project

Experiment to see whether spiracles help a grasshopper to float.

Materials

- Paper, plastic, or Styrofoam™ cups
- Blunt-ended skewer or needle to poke holes
- Sink or large basin of water
- Illustration of grasshopper body showing spiracles

Directions

1. Study the spiracles on an illustration of a grasshopper. Which spiracles allow air in and which ones allow air out?

2. Form a hypothesis related to whether the spiracles on the grasshopper's body affects its ability to either float or drown.

3. Using one cup and a skewer or blunt needle, pierce four holes along the bottom edge of a cup. These will act as the four holes that allow air/water in.

4. Using just a touch of force (to simulate a grasshopper jumping into water) place the cup in a sink or basin of water and see what happens. Repeat the experiment, but pierce holes around the middle of the cup. How does the location of the air holes affect the ability to float or sink? Draw conclusions about what would happen to a grasshopper—whose spiracles are located on the lower part of its body—if it landed in water.

Grasshopper Quizzzzz

How much do you know about grasshoppers? Take this TRUE-FALSE quiz and find out! Place a ✔ under TRUE or FALSE. If you are not sure of the answer you may look it up.

	True	False
1. Grasshoppers can jump about ten times the length of their bodies.	☐	☐
2. Grasshoppers can change colors depending on their surroundings.	☐	☐
3. Grasshoppers make good swimmers.	☐	☐
4. Lizards, snakes, birds, and mice are enemies of the grasshopper.	☐	☐
5. Grasshoppers can defend themselves by biting.	☐	☐
6. The antennae on a grasshopper's body allow it to breathe.	☐	☐
7. Grasshoppers are related to crickets.	☐	☐
8. A green grasshopper is easy to see in a meadow.	☐	☐
9. Spiracles on the grasshopper's body help it to float.	☐	☐
10. Grasshoppers can destroy crops of corn and cotton.	☐	☐
11. People can jump 20 times their length like a grasshopper.	☐	☐
12. Some insects like to capture and eat grasshoppers.	☐	☐
13. A grasshopper has five eyes.	☐	☐
14. Grasshoppers may spit a brown liquid when they are handled.	☐	☐
15. Grasshoppers shed their skin, or molt, like snakes do.	☐	☐

Name _____

Fireflies

Information

A firefly is any member of a particular family of soft-bodied beetles known for producing a glowing or flashing light. Fireflies are also known as *lightning bugs*.

Fireflies lay eggs in moist places or in the ground. The eggs hatch into larvae that cannot fly but do glow. At this stage they are known as *glowworms* and take about two years to develop. Then there is a brief pupa stage when they change into adults.

Adult fireflies live between five and 30 days. It is only in these final few weeks of a two-year life span that a firefly can fly and flash light as an adult beetle. Most of its life is spent hidden in a form that does not even closely resemble its final stage as an adult firefly.

Project

Create a chart or booklet describing the sequence of the development of a firefly from egg to adult.

Materials

- *Fireflies* by Joanne Ryder
- Index cards   • Glossary
- How Does A Glowworm Grow? following
- Scissors   • Glue   • Stapler
- Construction paper for booklets and charts

Directions

1. Using index cards and the glossary, create vocabulary cards to use in understanding the terms: nymph, larva, pupa.

2. Read *Fireflies* to learn about the life of a firefly from the time it is a glowworm to its final days as an adult light-flashing firefly. (This is a book for young readers but is a valuable story to read aloud to older children. If it is unavailable, discuss the development of a firefly with the class.)

3. Reproduce How Does A Glowworm Grow? on which the steps are in a mixed-up order. Read captions and study illustrations. Starting at the box numbered "1," continue to number each box in order from 2 to 9 to show and describe the sequence of development. (Do this activity as a class, stopping after each step to be sure all students have the correct answer before continuing.)

4. Cut out the nine boxes and rearrange them in sequential order to show the development of a firefly. Create a chart or booklet to present your finished sequence, or create another format of your choice.

Answers: 2 9 6
                    3 8 4
                    7 1 5

How Does a Glowworm Grow?

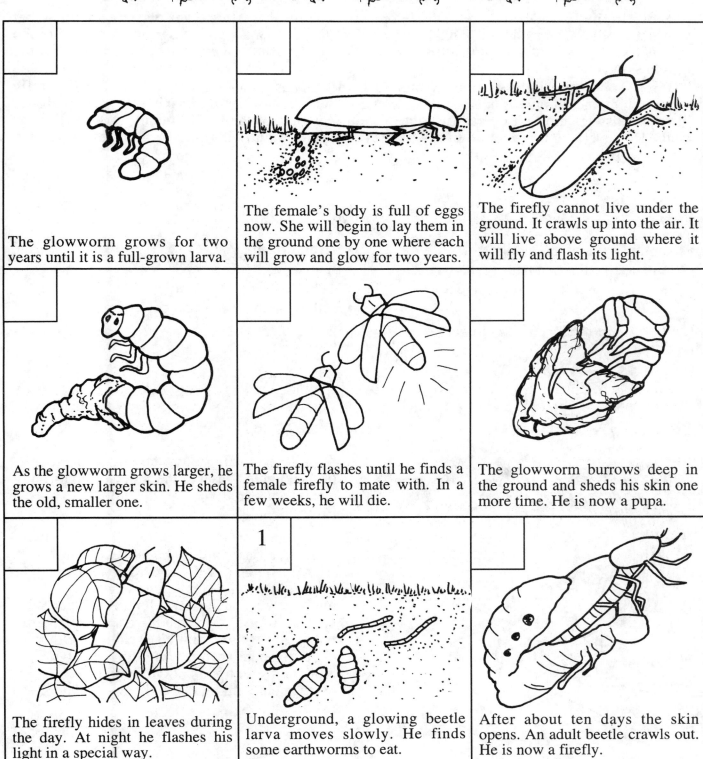

The glowworm grows for two years until it is a full-grown larva.

The female's body is full of eggs now. She will begin to lay them in the ground one by one where each will grow and glow for two years.

The firefly cannot live under the ground. It crawls up into the air. It will live above ground where it will fly and flash its light.

As the glowworm grows larger, he grows a new larger skin. He sheds the old, smaller one.

The firefly flashes until he finds a female firefly to mate with. In a few weeks, he will die.

The glowworm burrows deep in the ground and sheds his skin one more time. He is now a pupa.

The firefly hides in leaves during the day. At night he flashes his light in a special way.

Underground, a glowing beetle larva moves slowly. He finds some earthworms to eat.

After about ten days the skin opens. An adult beetle crawls out. He is now a firefly.

Bioluminescence

Information

Most fireflies produce light in their abdomen. A chemical reaction takes place in an organ that creates a heat-less, or cold light. This light is called *bioluminescence*. The light-making part of the body is like a flashlight. Behind the light is a reflector. In front is a clear, transparent area for the light to shine out.

Fireflies use their lights to find a mate. Each species has its own light signal. A female firefly may perch on the ground or in a bush and wait until a male flies nearby flashing the correct signal. She then answers him with her own light. Not all members of the firefly family give off light as adults. However, the larvae of all firefly species do give off light. This may be why they are known as glowworms.

Project

- Examine parts of a flashlight.
- Simulate fireflies sending light signals.
- Create firefly art using reflective art.

Materials

- Several flashlights
- Black construction paper
- Multi-colored glitter crayons
- Yellow neon pastels and colored pencils
- Scissors
- Paste

Directions

1. Working in small groups, take apart the tops of flashlights. Observe the reflector, bulb, and clear, transparent top parts. Compare to a firefly.

2. Make the room as dark as possible. Give two children a flashlight each and have them simulate a male firefly signaling a female firefly. One child (male firefly) creates a unique signal such as two long flashes and one short flash or by making a special pattern like a figure eight with his flashlight. Other child responds by repeating the light signal. Allow different pairs of children to experiment with unique light signals and be fireflies.

Firefly Art

Using black construction paper and reflective, neon, and glittery art materials create a scene showing fireflies in the night sky.

Use materials such as Crayola™ glitter-crayons, Prismacolor™ yellow neon colored pencils, bright yellow chalk and pastels to draw fireflies directly onto black paper. Covering the same area several times will create more intense color, and turning the black paper back and forth in the light may make it twinkle and shine! Show fireflies making their special light signals. Add 3-D folded green construction-paper leaves where female fireflies may be perched for added effect.

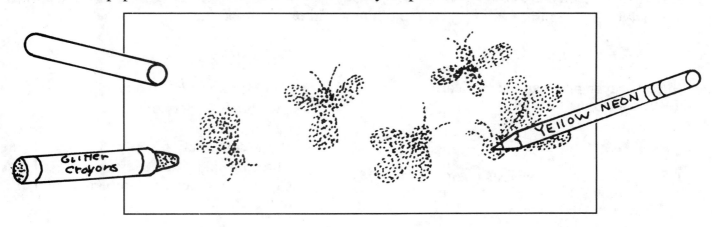

Cut out fireflies from neon day-glo yellow paper. Fold up wings and paste onto black construction paper. Add 3-D paper leaves and a moon and stars for an evening sky.

Did you know…? In some very hot climates, fireflies have lights in their thorax as well as in their abdomen and produce a very bright light. People catch them, put them in little cages and use them for lanterns. The glow can last for about two hours!

Ladybugs

Information

A ladybug is a small beetle with a round body shaped like half a pea. Usually it is bright red or yellow with black, red, white, or yellow spots.

The ladybug's hard back is really a pair of special front wings called *elytra*. These wings make a strong shield to protect the ladybug. When a ladybug wants to fly, the wings swing out to the sides. They do not flap, but they do help lift the ladybug into the air.

Ladybugs gather together in large numbers to hibernate through the winter. They leave their summer feeding grounds and seek shelter together in barns, cellars, attics, holes in trees, burrows, and other protected areas.

Ladybugs live in nearly every region of the world except in oceans.

Project

Make a paper-plate ladybug to learn about a ladybug's anatomy.

Directions

1. Hold one plate—convex side up—and cut a small section away at the top. Save this piece.

2. Cut the remaining large piece down the middle to form the wings. Color the two halves red, using paint, markers, or crayons.

3. Cut six or seven small black circles from the construction paper. Glue them onto the wings in a symmetrical pattern.

4. Place the two wings over the second plate (the body), convex sides up. Use brads to attach the upper corner of each wing to the body.

5. Color the reserved piece from step #1 black or black and white. Glue it to the body above the wings.

6. Cut three pipe cleaners in half for six legs. Fold them to resemble ladybug legs. Staple or glue three legs to each side of the body.

Materials

- Two paper or plastic picnic plates
- Two brads   • Scissors
- Glue or stapler
- Black construction paper
- Three black pipe cleaners
- Crayons, markers, or tempera paint in red and black

The Ladybug Story

Information

"The Ladybug Story" is the story of a second-grade class that worked with the lengthy legislative process to make the ladybug the state bug of Massachusetts! Read this fascinating and exciting story on the Internet. It tells every step of what the class had to do to get their bill passed.

Connect to the Internet and go to the Infoseek search engine. Search: ladybugs. Click on: "The Ladybug Story" by William Francis Galvin, Secretary of the Commonwealth, Tours and Government Education, Boston, Mass. Discuss the process the class went through to get the bill approved and passed. What conclusions can be drawn about why the legislators voted in favor of passing this bill. Discuss the reasons legislators would vote in favor of making the *mosquito* a state bug. Give reasons to support answers.

Project

Select an official insect to represent your state or province.

Materials

• Resource books
• Paper
• Pencils
• Poster board
• Art media of choice
• Computer, access to the Internet

Directions

1. Conduct research about insects that are native to your area.

2. Create a mock letter to your state or provincial government supporting your findings. Be sure to make scientific references.

3. Run a short school-wide campaign lobbying for its adoption. Create posters and banners to build support.

Aphid Eaters

Information

Ladybugs are considered beneficial insects. As predators they eat several kinds of crop-destroying insects. Ladybugs are voracious eaters of aphids (or plant lice) that destroy many kinds of plants. Gardeners especially like ladybugs for this reason and may put "lures" out to attract aphid-hungry ladybugs.

People who grow fruit and plants commercially often use ladybugs to control crop-damaging insects. They will buy thousands of ladybugs and release them over a period of time to eat the insects that are destroying their crops.

Sometimes ladybugs come into people's homes and become a pest. But people don't like to harm ladybugs because they are so helpful.

Project

- Conduct an experiment to see if ladybugs will eat things other than aphids.
- Follow the 100-A-Day Diet to demonstrate how much ladybugs can eat.

Materials

- Glass jars
- Paper towels
- Ladybugs
- Paint brush
- Lettuce, dead insects
- 100-A-Day Diet page, following
- Cotton swabs
- Cheesecloth
- Twigs with aphids
- Rubber band

Directions

Aphids are a ladybug's favorite meal. Will they eat anything else?

1. Find a ladybug and put it in a jar. Add a wet cotton swab or piece of wet paper towel. DO NOT put a water dish in as ladybugs may drown. They can easily suck the moisture they need from the swab or towel. Add a twig covered with aphids, or brush aphids off the twig into the jar with a paintbrush. Add tiny pieces of lettuce and one or two dead bugs. DO NOT include rocks, soil, or twigs as ladybugs may get crushed.

2. Cover the jar with cheesecloth and secure with a rubber band. Monitor daily as you add aphids and water. Are the ladybugs eating the lettuce or other insects? Try adding other foods. Draw conclusions about a ladybug's diet from the observations you make.

3. Reproduce 100-A-Day Diet page. Follow the instructions to experience how many aphids a ladybug can eat.

100-A Day Diet

One ladybug can eat as many as 100 aphids a day. Aphids are found on the underside of leaves on many plants and reproduce very quickly, so ladybugs rarely go hungry! What can you eat 100 of in one day? Brainstorm a list of possible answers. Using the chart below, and selecting a different item every day, keep a record of what you were able to eat. If possible, glue or tape a sample of the food item you selected each day in the appropriate box.

On Monday I ate 100 _____.

On Tuesday I ate 100 _____.

On Wednesday I ate 100 _____.

On Thursday I ate 100 _____.

On Friday I ate 100 _____.

Mosquitoes

Information

Mosquitoes are best known as pesky insects that thrive in warm, humid climates and bite humans and animals. Some mosquitoes carry germs of serious diseases.

Only the female mosquitoes "bite." They sip blood from victims which they need for the development of eggs inside their bodies. However, mosquitoes do not really "bite" because they cannot open their jaws. Their "bite" is really a stab through the victim's skin with six needlelike parts called *stylets*. Saliva flows into the wound through channels in the stylets.

Most people are allergic to the saliva and an itchy welt known as a "mosquito bite" forms. After the mosquito has sipped enough blood, it pulls the stylets out of the wound and flies away.

Project

Experiment with different repellents to draw conclusions about their effectiveness.

Directions

1. Brainstorm a list of how students treat their mosquito bites at home. What works well? What doesn't? Make a list of all responses.

2. Reproduce and distribute copies of the "Don't Bug Me" page and discuss the remedies suggested there. Take part in a class experiment to see which of the suggested new ideas works.

3. Depending on the season and your region, the experiment may be timely. If not, send the letter home and ask parents to list remedies they have found most successful in the past.

4. Compare results of what worked best. What conclusions can you reach about why this method worked well? Why do you think some other methods did not work effectively?

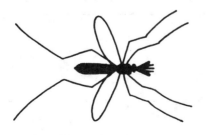

Materials

• Lemon juice, vinegar, peppermint oil
• Soap and water
• Ice
• Epsom salts
• Hot water
• "Don't Bug Me" parent letter, following

Don't Bug Me

Dear Parents,

As part of our study on insects, we are now learning about mosquitoes.

We invite you to take part in a class experiment. We would like to see if some unusual or different methods are helpful in remedying the itch of a mosquito bite and in repelling mosquitoes from biting at all.

The next time anyone in your family goes out on a day when mosquitoes are likely, ask them to tie a strip of Bounce™ fabric softener to their belt. As reported by Florida residents, it is believed that the scent helps keeps mosquitoes at bay. This is not a scientific finding, but we would like to see if it works for you.

Here are some anti-itch suggestions to try the next time a mosquito is successful in biting someone in your family. Please mark what was effective, what was not, and what you didn't try.

We appreciate your input and we will let you know the results of this class experiment. Thank you!

Teacher

Anti-itch Remedies	Worked Well	Didn't Work Well	Didn't Try
Lemon juice			
Vinegar			
Peppermint oil			
Epsom salts/hot water			
Anti-bite Remedies			
Bounce™ fabric softener			
Onion juice			

Mosquito—"Little Fly"

Information

Mosquitoes are flies since they are insects with two wings instead of four like most other insects. The word *mosquito* means "little fly" in Spanish.

Most kinds of mosquitoes are ⅛ to ¼ inch (3 to 6 mm) in length. Considering its tiny size, it causes big problems. Scientists continue to study new and effective ways to control the mosquito population. One study used fish that eat mosquito larvae to keep them from reproducing. If you live in an area with mosquitoes, you know scientists still have a lot of work to do!

Mosquitoes have a short life-span. Females live about 30 days and males live only between seven and ten days.

Project

Complete a puzzle to match answers to questions about mosquitoes.

Materials

- Mosquito Puzzlers page, following
- Resource books
- Cardboard for puzzle backing
- Scissors
- Paste or glue
- Zip-top plastic bags

Directions

1. Reproduce the puzzle page. (It's a good idea to reproduce each copy onto a different-colored paper so puzzle pieces are easy to sort.)

2. Spread paste or glue over entire sheet of cardboard and affix the puzzle page to it. Press it firmly in place, checking that all edges are secure. Allow it to dry.

3. When dry, cut the puzzle pieces apart. Place each individual puzzle in a zip-top plastic bag.

4. Use resource books to solve the puzzles independently or in groups.

Mosquito Puzzlers!

Do mosquitoes take blood only from humans?

No! They'll go after mammals, birds, and reptiles, too.

Where do mosquitoes lay their eggs?

Usually in standing water.

Do mosquitoes migrate?

They can only fly about 2 ½ miles in one hour so they don't travel very far.

Where do mosquitoes spend the winter?

They hide out in barns, caves, tree holes, and cellars.

How large is a mosquito's brain?

About this size .

About how many mosquitoes are there in one pound?

About 20,000.

Mosquitoes prey on us. What preys on them?

Bats, birds, other insects, lizards, spiders, fish, and US!

Why do mosquitoes bite some people more than others?

They smell better!

Do mosquitoes help in any way?

They help to pollinate flowers.

Flies

Information

A fly is an insect with one pair of well-developed wings. The common house fly is one of the best known kinds of flies, but black flies, fruit flies, gnats, horse flies, mosquitoes, and tsetse flies are also very familiar types.

Some flies are dangerous in addition to being a pest. They carry germs inside their bodies as well as on their bodies. When a fly touches an object, it may leave some germs behind.

Flies are among the fastest of all flying insects. A house fly can fly about 4.5 miles (7.2 km) per hour. The buzzing sound of a fly is made by its wings beating; a house fly's wings beat about 200 times per second! In place of a second set of wings, flies have *halteres* that keep them in balance and allow them to dart in any direction.

Project

- Make a fly swatter to use with experiments in flight patterns of flies.
- Research for fly facts and figures.

Directions

1. Place the netting or mesh piece on a desk or table.

2. With adhesive side of tape facing down, run the tape along one side of the netting with only half the width on the tape. Press firmly into place and cut at the corner.

3. Turn the netting over and press the remaining width of the tape onto the other side.

4. Repeat on all four sides. Trim corners.

5. With adult supervision, attach the swatter to a paint stirrer with a strong stapler.

4. Use the fly swatters in an observation activity:
   - Go outside and find a fly or find one inside the classroom.
   - Quietly observe the fly's activity. How long does it sit quietly? Does it seem to sense when something approaches?
   - Without touching the fly, use the fly swatter to make a noise or to fan air toward the fly and observe its reaction.
   - Draw conclusions about the fly's ability to sense movement.

6. Use resource books to complete the answers to Fly Facts and Figures.

Materials

- Paint stirrer • Scissors • Stapler
- Stiff netting or mesh—with small openings—cut into four-inch (10-cm) squares
- One-inch (2.5-cm) masking tape or colored shop tape
- Fly Facts and Figures page, following
- Resource books

Answer Key for page 35: 1. 13.5 (21 km), 31.5 (50 km), 45 (72 km), 63 (101 km) 2. 2,000, 6,000, 12,000, 24,000 3. 100,000 4. one-twentieth of an inch (1.3 mm) 5. 3 inches (7.6 cm), 3 inches (7.6 cm) 6. Four, egg, larva, pupa, adult 7. One, 250, 1,000 8. Eight, 30 9. 21 10. Eight, two

Fly Facts and Figures

1. House flies fly an average of 4.5 miles (7.2 km) per hour. How far would a fly go in:

   three hours? _____ seven hours? _____ 10 hours? _____ 14 hours? _____

2. A house fly's wings beat about 200 times per second. How many times would a fly's wings beat in:

   ten seconds? _____ 30 seconds? _____ one minute? _____ two minutes? _____

3. There are about _____ kinds of flies.

4. Flies live throughout the world. Some of the smallest are midges known as no-see-ums. They are about _____ long and are found in forests and marshes along coasts.

5. One of the largest flies, the mydas fly, is found in South America. It is _____ long and measures _____ from the tip of one wing to the tip of the other.

6. A fly's life is divided into _____ stages. They are _____, _____, _____, and _____.

7. A female fly lays from _____ eggs to _____ eggs at a time depending on the species of fly. During her lifetime, a female fly may produce as many as _____ eggs.

8. A house fly's eggs hatch in _____ to _____ hours.

9. Adult house flies live about _____ days in the summer. They live longer in cool weather, but are less active. Most adult flies die when the weather gets cold; however, some hibernate. Many larvae and pupae stay alive during the winter and then develop into adults in the spring.

10. A fly breathes through air holes called spiracles located along the sides of its body. The abdomen has _____ pairs of spiracles, and the thorax has _____ pairs.

Source: *World Book*   Name _____

Focus on Flies

Information

A fly's body has some unique features. It has sticky feet and claws that enable it to walk upside-down on the ceiling or on smooth, slippery surfaces such as glass and mirrors. Like some other insects, it can taste with its feet.

A fly's eyes are made up of hundreds of tiny lenses. When a fly sees something, it is broken up into many, many tiny pieces like a mosaic.

The wings of a fly are so thin that the veins show through. The veins help to stiffen and support the wings.

Flies like to warm their bodies in the sun. The hairs on their bodies help take in the heat.

Project

Make a mosaic of a fly as if you were seeing through the eyes of a fly.

Directions

1. Cut construction paper and waxed or tissue paper into small square pieces for mosaic work.

2. Duplicate the Mosaic Fly pattern onto white construction paper. Working one section at a time, spread glue onto the pattern. Place black construction paper squares onto the pattern, leaving narrow spaces between the pieces to create a mosaic effect. Do NOT cover the wings with black paper.

3. Glue black pipe cleaners over the legs on pattern and cut to length.

4. Working one section at a time, spread glue onto the wings and place waxed paper or white tissue paper squares in the same way. Allow it to dry.

5. With the narrow-tipped red marker, trace over the vein lines in the wings.

6. Mount the finished work onto cardboard or poster board.

7. Create a bulletin board display. Add a chart highlighting the unique body features of a fly as mentioned above.

Materials

- Mosaic Fly pattern, following,
- Black and white construction paper
- Waxed paper or white tissue paper
- Black pipe cleaners
- Narrow-tipped red marker
- Cardboard or poster board
- Scissors   • Glue

Mosaic Fly

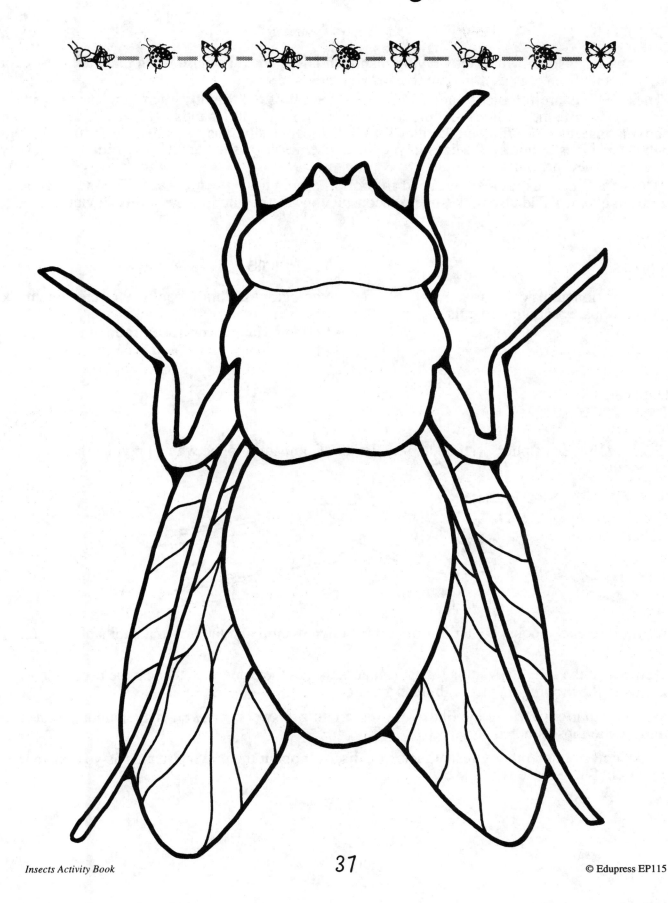

Praying Mantis

Information

A mantid is also known as the praying mantis. It is so named because when it is out hunting for food, it lifts its front legs as if it were in a praying position.

These insects are ferocious carnivores and not at all of the "saintly" demeanor as their name suggests. Their name should be "preying mantis." A praying mantis will attack and devour venomous insects and will even eat its own kind. It can easily clasp an insect with its front legs which have spines or hooks. It seizes its prey in a viselike grip as it tears it apart with its jaw. They prefer to eat their prey alive.

Almost all mantids are camouflaged to look like brown or green foliage. This helps conceal them from enemies and also makes them inconspicuous as they lie in wait for insect victims.

Project

Use observation and a comparison chart to compare a praying mantis to other insects.

Materials

- Photographs, library books, and reference books on other insects
- Praying Mantis worksheet, following
- Pliers

Directions

1. Practice the use of pliers to hold an item firmly. Compare it to the way a praying mantis holds its victims.

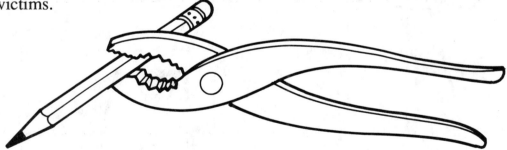

2. Using reference books, gather information about a mantid and the unusual habits of this greedy insect.

3. Reproduce the Praying Mantis worksheet and discuss the categories that can be used to compare the praying mantis with other insects.

4. Divide into groups to use the library for researching answers. Answers may include insects in addition to those studied so far.

5. Make notes of any other unusual facts you discover about the praying mantis as you do your research. Share these with the class.

Praying Mantis

The praying mantis is a most unusual insect. It has some habits and features of other insects but behaves somewhat differently. Read, research, and write your answers to compare the praying mantis to other insects.

	Praying Mantis	**Other Insect Name:**
What does it eat?		
How does it protect itself?		
Does it eat its prey alive or kill it first?		
In what areas of the world does it live? What climate conditions does it like?		

What other interesting fact did you find?

Dragonflies

Information

A dragonfly is a beautiful flying insect with four fragile and delicate wings that resemble fine gauze. The body is long and slender and may be a variety of colors with black markings. Large bead-like eyes cover most of the head.

As it flies, it holds its six legs together like a small basket and uses it to hold insects it captures such as mosquitoes and gnats. The dragonfly eats them as it flies and makes room for more in the basket.

Dragonflies have been known to fly 50-60 miles (80-97 km) an hour. This speed helps them to escape from birds or other insects.

Project

- Visit a pond and learn the role that dragonflies play in a pond's ecosystem.
- Create an insect aquarium.

Materials

- Books and photographs
- Buckets
- Small nets
- Materials for insect aquarium: glass bowl, small pebbles, dead branches, waterweed, tadpoles or raw fish (for food)

Directions

1. Invite children who have gone fishing in a pond to tell what else they have seen in ponds (flatworms, diving beetles, dragonfly larvae, other insects).

2. If possible, visit a natural pond. Ponds that have a lot of plant life will have more kinds of insects than ponds with little vegetation. Bring a pail and take turns scooping up samples of pond life. (If necessary, you may be able to find pond life samples in pet stores, the science department of local colleges, universities, or a school district science center).

3. If you are fortunate and capture a dragonfly nymph, bring it back to class and set up a pond aquarium. The nymph is a fierce underwater predator as it captures insect larvae, worms, and small animals in the pond. (They can swim underwater as they breathe with gills in the ends of their abdomens.)

4. To set up a pond aquarium for a dragonfly nymph, you will need a large glass bowl placed near sunlight but protected from direct sunlight. Collect materials listed above from a pond or river and rinse everything off before placing it in the aquarium.

5. The dragonfly nymph remains in the water for one to five years. It would be ideal to capture a nymph when it is fully developed in order to see it emerge.

6. If you place different kinds of insects in your aquarium, they may eat one another. Put some waterweed in it to provide hiding places.

A Dragonfly Emerges

When a dragonfly *nymph* has fully developed, it leaves the pond for the first time in its life. It climbs onto a branch or plant stem above the surface of the water and soon a change begins to take place. The old skin splits down the back and the adult's body begins to emerge—first the head, then the thorax with its long legs and crumpled wings, and finally the abdomen. Within hours, the wings harden and dry and are full size. The adult is ready to begin the final phase of its life—out of the pond and in the air.

Observe a Dragonfly Emerge. If you have a dragonfly nymph that has grown large and has stopped eating, it will soon begin to emerge. Put a dead branch in the aquarium. Be sure that it is set firmly in pebbles and sticks out of the water so the dragonfly can hold on to it as it emerges. When the nymph begins climbing the branch, darken the room. Wait quietly and patiently and observe as the adult dragonfly begins to emerge.

You may also try to observe a dragonfly emerge in its natural setting as it leaves the water and climbs onto a rock. An adult dragonfly will live for only a few weeks to a few months.

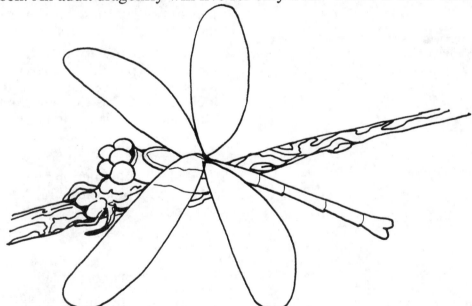

Divide into groups to research and answer these questions. Share group answers.
- How does the dragonfly help the ecosystem of a pond? What does it eat? What preys on the dragonfly?

- Natural ponds are sometimes hard to get to because of cattails and other plants surrounding it. What is another way to visit a pond?

- What are other names that dragonflies are sometimes called?

Caterpillars

Information

A caterpillar is the second, or *larval*, stage in the life cycle of butterflies and moths. A butterfly egg hatches; a tiny caterpillar crawls out and begins to eat and eat and eat. All of its growing takes place in this caterpillar/larval stage. As it grows, the caterpillar gets too big for its skin. It grows a new, larger skin and sheds the old one several times.

When the caterpillar has grown to a sufficient size and the season is right, it becomes a *pupa* (or *chrysalis*). The caterpillar changes into a butterfly and its wings form.

When the butterfly first emerges from its chrysalis, it rests in the sun until its wings are dry and they are firm enough to hold up.

The length of each stage in the cycle depends on the type of butterfly and where it lives.

Project

Create a folded-paper caterpillar to learn about a caterpillar's body.

Materials

- Yellow construction paper cut into 12 x 36 inch (8 x 91.5 cm) strips (two strips per child)
- Black construction paper
- Scissors
- Paste or stapler
- Pipe cleaners
- Markers
- Pictures of caterpillars

Directions

1. Look at pictures of caterpillars to identify features. Describe a caterpillar's body: 13 segments plus the head; a pair of legs attached to each of the first three segments*; four or five pair of prolegs on the abdomen**, six eyes on each side of the head; a pair of short feelers.

2. Distribute two strips of yellow construction paper to each child if you have 36-inch paper. If not, attach two 18-inch strips to form each 36-inch strip. Place strips at right angles to each other and glue or staple in place. Fold one strip over the other continuously and glue or staple ends together. Cut off excess.

3. Add black construction paper legs and create feelers with pipe cleaners. Add eyes with markers.

*The legs just behind the head are called true legs because they become the legs of the butterfly.

**The stumpy legs in the middle and at the end are prolegs or false legs. They disappear in the pupa stage.

Move Like a Caterpillar

Caterpillars usually have eight pairs of legs. The thin, clawed legs located just behind the head are called *true legs* because it is these that become the legs of a butterfly. The stumpy legs growing in the middle and the pair at the tail end are called *prolegs* or *false legs* because these legs disappear in the pupa stage.

Move like a caterpillar! Go to an indoor gymnasium or other large room with ample floor space for everyone to move around easily on. Divide into three teams: measuring worms, yellow-necked caterpillars, and slug caterpillars. Each group attempts to duplicate the movement of their team-named caterpillar.

Measuring Worms or Inchworms

This caterpillar family has no middle legs. When these caterpillars crawl, they hump their bodies up in the air and then lift their hind legs to meet their front ones. This movement is similar to a baby moving across the floor using its hands and feet, moving both hands at once and then both feet instead of moving with hands and knees. As these caterpillars loop along a twig or branch, it appears as if they are measuring it.

Yellow-Necked Caterpillars

Another caterpillar family has middle legs but no hind ones. They hold up their tails and wave them around. When they are frightened, they do a back bend until their heads and tails are almost touching.

Slug Caterpillars

In place of legs, these caterpillars have sucker-like pads on their undersides. Instead of crawling, they appear to ripple across the surface of a leaf. Their form of locomotion, or movement, is more like a snail or a slug than a caterpillar.

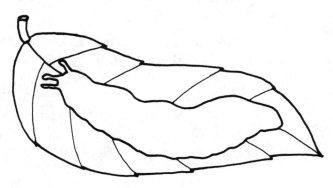

Butterflies

Information

Butterflies have one of the most dramatic life cycles in the insect world. They go through a complete *metamorphosis* from egg to caterpillar to chrysalis to butterfly.

Butterflies have two pairs of wings that operate like a single pair as they are closely linked. The surface of the wings is made up of thousands of tiny overlapping scales similar to the tiles on a roof. The scales give off a special scent called a *pheromone* to attract the opposite sex.

Most butterflies feed on the nectar of particular flowers, but some eat fruit, sap from trees, or the sticky fluid made by aphids. They have a long hollow feeding tube called a *proboscis* which is similar to a drinking straw. Butterflies uncoil it to reach into flowers and sip the nectar.

Project

- Examine a butterfly's wings with a magnifying glass.
- Make a butterfly mask and sip nectar.

Directions

1. Using a magnifying glass, examine a butterfly's wings to see the tiny scales. Observe antennae used for smelling and the proboscis, which when uncurled, is used for sipping nectar and feeding.

2. Reproduce and distribute Butterfly Mask pattern. Trace it onto black construction paper and cut out.

3. Using small pieces of sponge and paint, dab bright colors onto the wings.

4. Allow to dry. Cut out two eye-holes. Punch holes at each end. Add ties made of string.

5. Pretend to be a butterfly. Pour samples of apricot, peach, and other flavored nectar drinks into small cups and sip through straws.

6. Display finished butterfly masks on the bulletin board with a chart showing the life cycle of a butterfly.

Materials

- Preserved butterflies
- Magnifying glass
- Butterfly Mask pattern, following
- Bright paint colors
- Sponges
- Scissors
- String
- Curly straws or flex-straws
- Apricot and peach nectar
- Small cups

Butterfly Mask

Insect Sleuths

There are over 800,000 kinds of insects in the world; this book has discussed ten. It's time to go out to see how many different insects you can find where you live. Brainstorm some places where insect-hunting might be most successful, then head out with magnifying glasses, trowels, and any other tools you think would be helpful. Remember—don't touch; leave the insects in their natural habitats. Watch carefully and see what you observe! Keep a tally of how many of each insect you found, recording where you found it. Can you find some that aren't found in the book? You may need to use an encyclopedia to identify your insects.

	Insect	Description	Where I found it
1			
2			
3			
4			
5			
6			
7			
8			
9			
10			
11			
12			
13			
14			
15			

Game Center

Use your knowledge about insects for outdoor fun!

Cricket Races

Preparation:
- Practice jumping skills, working to make long jumps without falling.
- Divide into teams of equal numbers. (If the numbers are not even, some teams members will have to race more than one time.)

To Play:
- Conduct a cricket race in which each team member jumps to a marked point, then back to his team.
- As an alternative, set up an obstacle course for the crickets to race through.

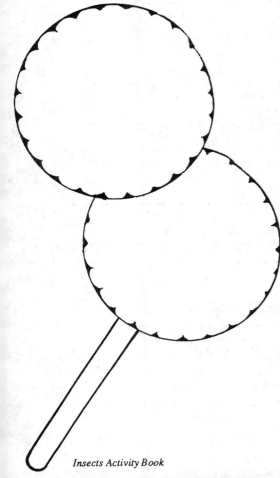

Firefly Scramble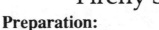

Preparation:
- Decide how many teams the class will divide into easily. (Two or three to begin with).
- Cut three-inch (7.6-cm) circles from white and yellow construction paper. You will need one of each color per person. Glue a white circle and a yellow circle back-to-back, with a craft stick in between them as a holder.
- Thinking of the yellow circles as light flashes, create a light-flashing pattern for each team. For example: flash, flash, pause for a count to five, flash. Write the pattern on an index card for each member of a team.

To Play:
- Mix up the index cards and distribute randomly. Explain what the terms on the cards mean: to make a flash, the yellow circle is turned to the front, then turned back.
- Players observe the flashing patterns of the other players, and try to recognize fireflies using the same pattern as themselves. When two players think they have a matching pattern, they pair up and start looking for other fireflies with the same flashing pattern. The goal is to gather together all the the fireflies within one team.

World Wide Web

A bug-jar and a magnifying glass aren't the only tools you can use for insect-hunting. Look in the world wide web to expand your knowledge of the world of insects. Keep in mind that web pages change constantly. The web pages below were active at publication date but their continued presence is not guaranteed. New, exciting sites are as numerous as the insects that live in this wide world!

Address	Content
www.eagle.ca/~matink/insects.html	*Insects*—A site designed to assist in research about insects. Lots of information and pictures. Includes many weblinks.
info.ex.ac.uk/~gjlramel/six.html	*Welcome to the Wonderful World of Insects*—Lots of fun and useful insect information.
kato.theramp.net/julian/insects.html	*Insects*—Database, information, and photographs of the world's insects.
www.luhsd.k12.ca.us/library/science/insects.html	*Insects*—Collecting, mounting, and identifying insects. Lots of weblinks and insect recipes.
home.eznet.net/~arnesp/insect.html	*Insect Activities*—Tips on bug-watching, insect identification, pictures. Lots of ideas for learning about bugs, having fun at the same time.